Carmel Reilly Karen Young

Australia • Brazil • Japan • Korea • Mexico • Singapore • Spain • United Kingdom • United States

Buzz Sees the Difference

Fast Forward
Purple Level 19

Text: Carmel Reilly
Illustrations: Karen Young
Editor: Johanna Rohan
Designer: Vonda Pestana
Series designer: James Lowe
Production controller: Seona Galbally
Audio recordings: Juliet Hill, Picture Start
Spoken by: Matthew King and Abbe Holmes
Reprint: Jennifer Foo

ISBN 978 0 17 012648 9
ISBN 978 0 17 012645 8 (set)

Cengage Learning Australia
Level 7, 80 Dorcas Street
South Melbourne, Victoria Australia 3205
Phone: 1300 790 853

Cengage Learning New Zealand
Unit 4B Rosedale Office Park
331 Rosedale Road, Albany, North Shore NZ 0632
Phone: 0508 635 766

For learning solutions, visit cengage.com.au

Printed in Australia by Ligare Pty Ltd
6 7 8 9 10 11 12 21 20 19 18 17

Evaluated in independent research by staff from the Department of Language, Literacy and Arts Education at the University of Melbourne.

Carmel Reilly

Karen Young

Contents

THE PEACE CONFERENCE

Buzz and Zip were at the beach when the president of planet Zero rang.

"I need you to represent planet Zero at the peace conference on planet Seven," he told them.

"Peace conference," said Buzz.
"I'm not sure ...
I don't really like ..."

"Yes, sir," said Zip, cutting off Buzz.
"That sounds great!
We'll get ready right away."

Two days later, Buzz and Zip
landed their spaceship
at the conference centre
on planet Seven.

Buzz grabbed Zip's arm.
"Look at that!" he said,
pointing to a four-headed
representative from planet Drill.

"Shh!" said Zip.

But Buzz wasn't listening.
He was now looking at a strange,
thin creature.
"That one's ugly!" he said.

"Will you be quiet?" Zip hissed.
"Everyone is different around here."

STRANGE CREATURES

Buzz and Zip followed the crowd across a square to a huge hall.
"I think I need something to eat," Buzz said as they were about to go inside.

"Buzz, this is a peace conference," said Zip.
"You need to start thinking about what we've all got in common."

Running Words 171

"Not much, by the look of them,"
said Buzz,
who was always in a bad mood
when he was hungry.

Buzz found a food stand
run by the representatives
from planet Juno.
The food looked very strange,
but tasted quite good.

Buzz took his food to the other side
of the square,
and sat down next to a wall.
He was happy to be away
from the crowds.

Suddenly, he heard a voice coming from the other side of the wall.

"Have you seen how hideous most of them are?" it whispered. "Just think how much better they'll look when we blow them up!"

THE BOMB

Buzz froze.
Finally, very quietly,
he slowly peered around the corner.
He saw two of the representatives
from planet Bang.
Buzz popped his head back
and sat very still.

"We'd better get out of here.
That bomb is set to go off
in ten minutes,"
said one of the representatives.

"Okay, let's go,"
laughed the other.

Buzz waited until they had gone.
Then, he leapt up and raced
into the hall.
As he ran in, he tripped on the stairs
and tumbled down.
He made so much noise
and everyone stared at him.

Finally, Buzz found his seat
next to Zip.
"Don't panic,
but there's a bomb in here!"
he whispered.

Zip looked at him and shook
his head.
"As if I believe that!
You would do anything
to get out of being here,
wouldn't you?"

Buzz could tell Zip would never believe him.
There was only one thing for him to do.

He leapt onto his desk
and starting screaming
and waving his arms.
"There's a bomb in here!
Run!"

Within seconds, there was a stampede as everyone rushed for the doors.

REACHING OUT

As the hall cleared,
Buzz saw the thin, strange creature from earlier.
He was still in his seat.
"Come on!" Buzz shouted to him.

But the creature didn't move.
It was wearing a sight and sound headset, and hadn't seen or heard what was going on.

Without thinking, Buzz ran down
to grab the creature.
But as he reached it,
he stopped and looked –
it really was the ugliest thing
Buzz had ever seen!

Buzz stood still.
He had never touched anything
like this creature before.
He took a deep breath,
reached up and shook
the creature's shoulder.

The creature pulled off its headset,
looked down at Buzz and smiled.
For some reason,
Buzz couldn't help smiling back.
"Come on," he said,
holding out one of his hands.
"We need to get out of here."

Chapter 5

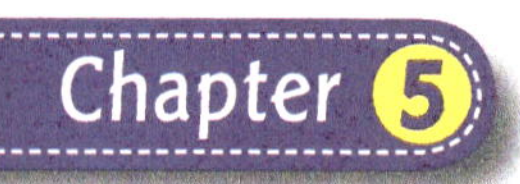

THE DIFFERENCE

Buzz and the creature dived for cover just as the bomb went off.
Bits of brick and dust flew everywhere.

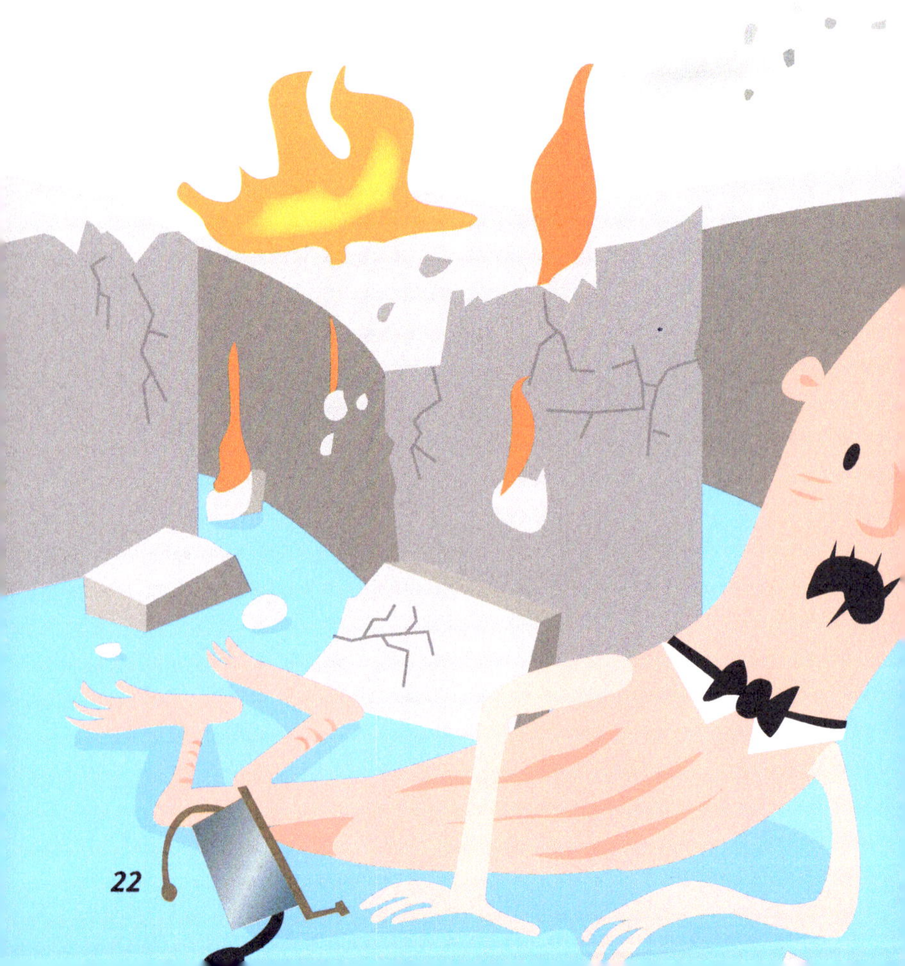

"I can't believe someone would bomb
a peace conference, just because
they didn't like the look of us,"
the creature said.
"I mean, you're hideous,
but I'm not going to let it worry me!"

Buzz's mouth dropped open.

Just then, Zip came towards them.
For the first time Buzz noticed
how different Zip was.
Zip looked as strange
as the creature standing beside him.
Well, almost, but not quite.

After all, Zip was Buzz's best friend.
He couldn't be that different,
could he?